'*The only reason Caroline wrote this book is to collect Menz Tearz (TM)*

in jars as they weep when they read it'

—   Sean Doyle,
philanthropist.

Fahckmylife 2: The Devil's Doorbell

by Caroline Egan

TaBlE oF cOnTeNtS

Thank you to all the people who backed my Indiegogo:

Cait McGrath

Martina Ferrari

Paul Cooke

Ann Fox

Elaine Egan

Michael Corrigan

Kevin McParland

Ben Crane

Averyl Quinn

Mark Murphy

Jack Moulder

Marie Kearns

James Connolly

(Your hand jobs are in the post – apart from you Elaine because obviously that would just be weird)

'Bitches ain't shit and they ain't saying nothing.

A hundred motherfuckers can't tell me nothing.'

\-   Nicki Minaj

Beez in The Trap, 2012

FoReWoRd

This book is a big mishmash of work mostly from the last two years
(with a little proceeding that), during various states of stress and
mess. It contains previously published work including *Every Night
They Came* (part of Phoenix Ink 5). It also has a reworked, more
realistic version, of an original story published on Left Hooks, now
called *Downloading An Abortion,* pre-dating the 8th's repeal here. Are
these real stories? You decide! I've also included some poetry and
amusing lists to keep the spirits up. To be fair, I could've gone mega
dark, but I tried to balance fun and making a point without getting
overly morose.

So, what's changed since the last book? Well on a larger scale the
8th was repealed here, but its full ramifications haven't been properly
yet because y'know… women aren't a priority… The #Metoo
movement became a thing… but can you really trust gold grabbing
women and ugly feminists though? The world is turning into a load
of burning plastic too… probably caused by plastic tampon
applicators but y'know… women, wha?

Like I know there's always a massive culture of fear generated by the
news, which has to an extent been compounded by social media.
Apparently millennials are way more likely to experience anxiety and
depression than previous generations, but not because we're
'snowflakes' (ugh.. so tired and overused) but because the
generations before us pretty much fucked us over. Not only that but
now, more than ever, opinions exist in simple black and white, and it
seems to me like everyone is defensive, angry, blamey and
frightened. Climate change, knickers used as evidence in a rape
case, the Catholic Church, Love Island, soaring rent prices, Brexit

and fake moral outrage at the suggestion (by nobody) of a gender neutral Santa (which dopes unquestioningly believe straight away) is just some of the bollox that we've had to deal with over the last year or so. Not to mention the fact that when people are actually even found guilty that their accountability and punishment are not being upheld.

If you're looking for life advice on how to deal with any of this you've probably come to the wrong place. To be honest cognitive dissonance is the easiest way to go, for your mental health alone. Although if you want to learn how to deal with being alive and anxious you might get something out of this. Or at least a laugh, right? We all need a laugh sometimes and maybe we all feel a little bit useless, because we there is so much that we can't control around us.

On a personal note, before I leave you with my self-indulgent ramblings, I'd like to share a little thing with you about how I've changed my mindset over the last two years. It may not work for you (if you even need it) but weirdly it did for me. People always talk about remaining positive and that if you project positive thoughts and energy out into the universe it will come back to you. If that works for you cool. But, honestly could you actually see me doing that? Nope. It could literally never be me. So what did I do instead?

I LIED.

I LIED CONSTANTLY TO MYSELF.

I LIED EVERY SINGLE DAY AND TOLD MYSELF THAT I WAS HAPPY.

I literally could have been on fire and I would've kept saying it.

When things got really hard for a while I said it even more to myself.
I lied and told myself I didn't care what people were saying about me
behind my back and that I was fine.

I lied and told myself that I was fun, that I wasn't a wreck and that my
life was full of opportunity.

I lied over and over and over.

The entire time I was lying I continued to take little baby steps to
improve my mental health, situation and myself.

LIES. LIES. LIES.

And then one it wasn't a lie any more. I was happy and I was more
together and didn't give a fuck about what anyone thought anymore.
And here we are, by no means perfect, but definitely improved.

Anyway, thank you for showing your support by reading this. I hope
you enjoy these bits and pieces nearly as much as I have writing
them.

EvErY nIgHt ThEy CaMe

Every night they came. Their little feet pattering gently on the laminate flooring, their tiny cold hands pulling at the end of his bed sheets and their barely audible whispers. Every night he pretended to be asleep, covering his blue eyes with his hands, his knuckles whitening, hidden in the sticky heat of his thick bed spread. He knew what they looked like, but, because seeing was believing, he had rathered not to reconfirm their existence.

If I can't see you it means you're not real.

Frozen in that same position every night, his pulse throbbing in his head, the boy often wondered what they had wanted. He tried to work through the situation as logically as any eight-year-old could. The fear he felt, that paralysing sense of powerlessness, took over every time, refusing to fade. His shivering body would not allow his mind to process thought as little fingers mauled the duvet inches from his arms.

If I can't see you, you can't see me.

Three weeks ago he had thought that his eyes were playing tricks on him. The shadows often had a way of morphing into fearful unknown creatures or concealing the cause of a suspicious sound. He had been convinced in the initial stages that it must be mice, possibly even rats, when he had heard the rustle and patter in the depths of his dark bedroom and felt the presence of a ball roll eerily across the floor towards his bed. It was only when he heard the indistinct whispers, the indecipherable meandering of a mad person on a mission, that he knew he could not deny his situation.

If I can't hear you then you're not here.

Despite his usual overwhelming terror the boy had plotted tiredly throughout the day. His teacher had commented to his mother recently that he had been falling asleep in class. His school work had, been deteriorating and he had developed dark circles under his eyes. The youthful glow of his face had been extinguished and replaced with the countenance of a war veteran that had seen too much. Even now, being a kid, he knew that this had to change. It had to end regardless of the consequence, and so, he devised a crude plan to make this a reality.

If I amn't here you can't get me.

He encountered one face to face in his narrow upstairs landing returning from the toilet, its silhouette stretching out in the pale moonlight from behind. It was a greyish brown colour and lacked expression, standing less than a foot tall in height. It blocked his passage with its narrow limbs and mimicked his every move. Like a plastic doll with gangly limbs its face was featureless bar its black eyes which blinked sporadically. It had no visible mouth, or nose, or ears, yet somehow regarded him menacingly. He froze to the spot and again it adapted his pose. It darted and dodged fluidly, never changing expression, its two toed feet tapping on the wood floor, until he ran back to the bathroom and locked himself in. The gentle scratching sound of the blunt nailless fingers followed a few minutes later.

If you can't touch me this isn't happening.

Now curled up in a tight foetal position the boy fingered a small object under his pillow. He would deal with this himself. Nobody would believe him. Grown-ups were pointless to talk to about it. He would never prove their existence, especially considering his recent odd behaviour, and even his brother at the age of eleven was closer to adulthood and their beliefs than he was. The whispering began to rise, as he contemplated this, and a newer stronger wave of fear climbed from the pit of his stomach upward, throwing his thoughts out of sync. Nobody else in the house could hear their terrifying malevolence either. They didn't even have mouths, so how could they whisper? Those horrible menacing thoughts. Mocking and planning…teasing and taunting…

If I don't think about it they will go away.

He had woken up on the bathroom floor the next morning, cold and sticky with puffy eyelids and a crust of dry drool on one side of his chin. The brightness of the room had stung his eyes and as he ran his hands through his wild blonde hair the nights' events began to replay in his mind. He wondered what they were. They seemed too artificial to be real: they were more man made than anything, like a deformed doll with no pupils. He wondered where they came from and what they wanted. He could come to no solid conclusion but he knew that it was unlikely to be good.

I'm in a happy place!

Sometimes the he had woken up feeling bruises throb on his arms and legs but when he looked for them he couldn't find them. He knew it had something to do with the creatures but there was nothing to see. So he decided to draw around where the pain was on his arm in pen to see what shape it was because he was a clever boy. His crudely traced drawing depicted something unsettling. It clearly showed the shape of a tiny hand, about the size of a golf ball. It seemed more as the result of a gentle touch as opposed to a slap, as if the creature had just put their hand on him. His body paralysed as he considered what this meant. When had they touched him?! Why hadn't he felt it?! Why were they doing this?!

If you don't see me then you're not real!

The boy rose slowly from the bed holding the matches tightly in his hands. It was nearly dawn and the room would start to become grey with dim light. They only came out in the darkness. He squeezed his eyes shut and inched his way across the bed. He knew his room so well that even in the dark he would be able to negotiate his way to the wardrobe and not need to open his eyes until the last minute. A silence hushed the room, no more whispering, no more movement, just the sound of the boy's breathing as he could feel all their eyes following him. He lowered himself down to the floor, feeling its coldness beneath his feet, and continued as if approaching a wild animal. No sudden movements, no obviously malicious behaviour and he thought he could pull it off.

If I'm careful they won't know.

He head realised where they slept that very day, whilst tiredly cleaning his room. It appeared that behind his wardrobe they had made an entrance to a cave that was confined to a section inside his wall.

When his favourite marble had rolled behind it he pulled it out from the wall and noticed a bedding of rags and hay covering where they slept. Being young and exhausted he pondered this all day before coming up with the simple plan of burning their next. He had to carefully execute a plan to even obtain the matches by distracting his mother in the kitchen to steal them. He even robbed fire lighters to ensure that everything would go up in flames.

Fire, fire, burning bright.

He bent down to retrieve the fire lighters and felt cold fingers, gently, almost affectionately stroke his arm. He refused to open his eyes. The wicked things would surely try to confuse him their steady gazes, and lunge on him. He fumbled loosely for each of them, until he had his small hand full. He slowly opened his eyes but did not look around. Trembling he lit a match, aware of the semi-circle of stares that surrounded him. As he approached the first fire-lighter with the match he felt something move to his left – one of the creatures shook its head gently as if to say 'no', the flame dancing in its eyes, basked in the pale and short lived light.

The match extinguished and so flustered the boy lit another.

He felt the circle grow tighter around him and anticipation choked in his throat. He could feel their movements not too far away, the air moving from their gentle motions.

HoW tO nOt SeEm LiKe A mEsS: tHe CoVeRt GuIdE To AdUlTiNg At ChRiStMaS

Let's face it, you're a bit of a train wreck at the best of times, well either that or you seem to have a cold black stone where your heart should normally be, but you hold your shit together pretty well considering most of the time. However, Christmas is coming and we all know that means alternating between being locked and having the fear – two of the most delicate and emotional states of being. Whatever it is that fucks with you this time of year you need to protect yourself and project at least a half decent image of the more together you – because let's face it, you're a shite human being and you're going to be plastered.

So, here's how:

Before drinking change your Facebook status privacy to 'just me'. Nobody wants to see 'fjsisneiejs' at 4.50am, a crazy long YouTube party or any of your thoughts on the year when you're locked. You won't even want to and it'll make your fear worse.

Delete toxic people's numbers out of your phone so you can't drink dial them or ring them when you have the fear.

Bring a toothbrush everywhere.

Don't pay for drugs. Just don't. By all means take them if you're offered them though and just buy someone a drink or some shit.

Don't ride people you know already or work with. In other words, don't shit where you eat. Ride a randomer on the sly or go on Tinder. Nobody will know your bizness then and you know you do your best work when you don't care about them anyway.

Dress well all the time. Treat every day like you're going to get the ride, even if you don't want to.

Arrive late and hopefully sober to things.

Remember to eat you fucking fool.

Laugh all the time. Fake laugh. Shake your head and laugh till the mess of your life fades into obscurity.

Move the bin beside the head of your bed.

Listen to EDM 24/7 – no sad shit.

Stay away from vodka and Southern Comfort – you know what they do to you!

Hide money on yourself in your bra so you can always get home.

Pack knickers

When you find yourself getting too thoughtful go into the toilet and watch 5 minutes of parody porn to laugh and sober up slightly.

Save your sadness for when you're on your own watching The Green Mile in your filthy pjs.

Buy yourself a present if you're not expecting gifts from anyone like a sex toy or more drink.

Surround yourself with people that are fun and who you think might like you but you're not sure. Then you won't have serious conversations and you won't find yourself staring sadly at the ground.

Ask your child for extra cuddles to make up for the general lack of affection in your life. Scare them slightly.

Get drunk really early on New Year's Eve, turn your phone off and fall asleep in your pants covered in crackers at 9pm.

Buy a good supply of hangovers cures and craft a fake human to hold out of pillows with a hand drawn face for when you have the fear.

Have a conversation with yourself in the mirror drunk when you're fixing your make up telling yourself 'you're a mess' till you find it hysterical.

Puff, puff, pass – you don't want to take a whitey.

Never dance. You're shit.

Write down three things you want to change for the new year, crumple the page up, set it on fire and laugh.

Get a go pro and attach it to yourself on nights out to do something creative with your nights out. Leave it a few weeks before reviewing the footage though.

Start toasts with 'here's to being a fucking mess!'

Bring a novelty item or conversation point out with in case you feel awkward and can't make conversation – I favour googly eyes. Then everyone can get involved and it feels like a conversation but the focus isn't you.

If you're mostly drunk and usually introverted you'll probably seem way more outgoing than you actually are – possibly even manic if you've been on a bender. Remember to spend time alone.

Bring baby wipes with you everywhere to freshen up your front bum, clean up after cocaine shits and to wipe up your mascara when you end up crying toilet cubicles.

Do not answer any messages after midnight – well, unless you want to get your hole – clearly answer them.

Or y'know, you could just not drink at Christmas and stay home spending time with your family?

LOL.

aNd ThAt BaBy GrEw Up To Be ALbErT EiNsTeIn – KeItH DuFfY aNd GeTtInG uP tHe DuFf

OK so I thought I could go with a different type of tale today, so sit back, grab a cup of tea or get comfortable hiding in the jacks in work, whilst I regale you with a story of a day in my life of yesteryear. 'Twas the summer of 2003, I was 21, on break from college before returning for my final year of my degree and working in town. This shop was a novelty shop, mainly for children, producing a variety of teddy bears on the site to the specifications of stupid little people. We put in hearts, voice boxes, stuffing, dressed them and gave them birth certificates. We smiled and joked with children and it was all really saccharin, but, for the most part I enjoyed it. It paid well, I liked sewing and some children were scared of balloons which amused me no end.

This particular day was a strange one for me. I hadn't been feeling well for the last while. I had been putting on weight despite being on a very strict diet composed mainly of Slimfast milkshakes. I was really annoyed at myself for being the ghastly weight of 9 stone (oh how I laugh now at that) and had pretty much been starving myself for the past few weeks. The night before I was tossing and turning and had barely slept and somewhere in the recesses of my brain fluttered a serious hidden pang of anxiety. It was only sitting at the table at the back of the shop at the sewing table, staring at the small wide-eyed fools screaming incoherent shite, that the realisation hit me of what this potentially could be and so frantically on the short morning break I ran to the pharmacy on the floor below. Ten minutes later I was staring at a positive response on the test in the toilets, barely able to breathe.

When I left the toilet, confused and a bit shell shocked, I stumbled aimlessly back onto the floor. A supervisor approached me and told me that I had to go to the RDS. Why? Because I had to dress up, with another guy, in a mascot outfit – the giant smelly girl teddy for a photo shoot. I would get paid extra. I complied barely saying a word, partially glad to get away from all the children on the shop floor and pretending to be happy – my resting bitch face game would have been too strong for the public today. I was kinda paralysed watching children with their sticky hands pick up teddies, drop lollies and somewhere I could smell a well filled nappy. So I went with the other guy to the RDS, making awkward small talk and trying not to have a mental breakdown.

The costume had never been washed. Not once. And the inside of the heavy plastic head smelled like twenty people's stale breath. It was claustrophobic and heavy with warm air, despite the large opening for the mouth and eyes. In order to walk I had to press my face up tightly to the inside of the head and peer out the mouth, which I could only imagine looked macabre, appearing as if I was trapped inside the bear being slowly digested. I wondered if I tried hard enough would the body digest the foetus, thought that was stupid and asked someone to align my head properly. The costume hung loosely around my body, but felt crusty and trapped the building heat around me. Was it always this warm in this suit or was I just panicking? I could feel sweat drip down my back but there was nothing I could do about it.

How the fuck was I going to have a child? What would I ever do with one? Surely, I'd accidentally break its neck the first time I held it? All I did was booze, work, study and sleep. I had nobody to answer to. I lived with my parents in a teenchy gaff. When the goldfish became a pain in the arse they were flushed down the toilet like (not me), so what would happen with a screaming baby? What about college? I wanted to do my thesis on the Alien series and the idea of babies as parasites and bodily autonomy – seemed fitting now.

I was ushered along by someone I couldn't see - an irritating hand between my shoulder blades - into a flurry of people. I couldn't turn because the costume didn't always move with me and it was hard to orientate myself in it, so as much as I wanted to I couldn't push their hand off.

'Don't talk at all' a voice said.

Journalists, photographers, some TV presenters I could recognise but not name…. and there he was Keith Duffy, in all his orangeness (ornateness kept coming up in spell-check as a possible correction and I can't stop laughing at it) with his crazy white teeth, standing smiling away in the middle of it all. It didn't matter that I could barely see out the mouth – I could still tell he was famous, even in his shit blue jumper. Other people dressed as teddies pranced around with exaggerated poses. It was like walking into a party where you were the only one who hadn't taken cocaine whilst everyone went all Scarface. He was moved over to me, the only female bear, and tightly wrapped his arm around my neck, as flashed went off. I tried to pose in some way enthusiastically and made eye contact with him through the mouth and he smiled in the most comforting way into the bears mouth. It must've looked super weird to him. It was, however, magical for me. We were sharing a moment.

Inside, still reeling from the news earlier, the heat rising and rising, I could feel myself start to have issues breathing. I could feel that it was possible that I would vomit inside the giant head as well, possibly morning sickness, possibly just from the stress of it. Thing is, although Keith was subconsciously calming me down, when you can't see anything in your peripheral vision you can be frightened easily. As he loosened his grip on me some squeaky gobshite jumped in front of me:

'*YOU'RE DEFINITELY A GUY!*' she squealed, not only giving me a shock but also causing me to back away slightly. '*YOU'RE DEFINITELY NOT A GIRL!*'

Over and over and over. Until warm and angry and panicked, the smelly girl bear shouted in front of the journalists, TV presenters and Keith Duffy.

'*I'M A FUCKING GIRL!*' I screamed.

Ten minutes later we were leaving on our way back to work, normal clothes but red faced, absolutely nothing acknowledged by anyone of my outburst, on the way to get a god-damn burrito. When my supervisor rang me to find out where we were – slightly angry I might add - I simply said in a narky tone 'to get a fucking burrito' and hung up. I was getting a burrito and I wasn't rushing it either.

Then in work I text the father of the child, not my partner at the time (long story) and told him we needed to chat. So yeah, I guess I had the kid but Keith Duffy also, without knowing it, stopped me having a panic attack.

EDIT: This story really did happen and I tried to Google pictures of me (as a bear) with Keith Duffy but I couldn't find any. If anyone does come across some please send them on! It'd be cool.

So YoU'rE wOrKiNg ClAsS nOw? – HoW tO dEaL wItH sUdDeNlY bEiNg pOoR iN DuBlIn.

I am working class and from Finglas. I may have moved around the country a lot (probably about 8 different houses before the age of 9) before we settled in Dublin in the early 90's but I consider Finglas my home. However, I was kind of in a weird situation, because I was never really considered middle-class or working class in any proper sense of the word. At various stages I was considered 'posh' as a disadvantage, was picked on in my area and in school and found it difficult to make friends in my area because my parents, who thought they were protecting me, wouldn't let me associate with people from my area. However, despite their best efforts and what-not I was still considered 'common' and likewise people weren't allowed to hang around with me. Also, I feel that the 'working class' label has worked to my disadvantage in college and lead to people severely underestimating me. So essentially I don't know what the fuck I am, although once I say Finglas with my glorious accent the decision is taken out of my hands. But I kinda dislike poshos anyway so I guess it doesn't matter.

Class is still a thing. There is elitism and there are still prevailing patronising attitudes towards people based on their 'class', which is now more complicated than ever to quantify, as if acquiring an education and being working class were a fucking oxymoron. I remember asking students during a tutorial whether they thought class was an issue and most of them replied that they didn't think that this was the case. They were all, however, at least middle-class so it probably is harder to see other people's difficulties when you're immersed in your own little bubble.

But even being middle-class is a precarious position now, as rent in Dublin has become a nightmare. If class is to be measured purely on occupation and income, as opposed to any other factors, there are more people who were possibly middle class falling closer towards the working-class tier than ever before. Sure, there might be jobs now, specifically in Dublin but rent is insane and capitalism is bullshit if you're not in the top 30%. For what has always been a struggle for some is now becoming more of a struggle for many people who had little understanding or compassion for those 'beneath them' on the food chain.

So, here are some tips on how to survive suddenly becoming working class:

Drink high percentage alcohol –the cheapest for the largest amount. You're poor so you're not allowed drink or have any fun, (see comments made by Senator David Norris the big posho) but without a temporary escape or whatever you've got fuck all to keep you in your downtrodden position.

If you're employed in a minimum wage job just be grateful that you even have one, even if you spent years in college studying things that are in no way related to what you are doing now. It's your own fault. Perhaps you were always born to be working class and no amount of denying it will help. The blue bloods say being poor is in the genes.

Get used to people telling you that the cost of living is way less in other locations in the country, despite the fact that Dublin is your home, and although rent is Dublin is a black hole and completely overpriced, they will completely overlook the long commute to a new job, or relocating your family, for what is essentially a catch 22 situation.

Don't have sex. Especially if you're a woman. Completely repress all needs and desires because if you get pregnant people will say that you only did it to get a house or a 'free ride' (pun intended) or if you have an accident and want to get it 'sorted' your options as a woman in Ireland are either extremely expensive or illegal. Remember don't have sex if you can't fully afford a child. Don't think that those affordable LIDL condoms will protect you.

Get used to the fact that it is property owners and the government in collusion with each other that could potentially make you homeless at any point and there is little recourse for you to follow up. Settle for squalor, damp and rats, landlords that follow their own rules and sewage leaking into your sitting room – because that actually happened to me before. (Seriously though leave refugees out of it. We have enough resources to look after everyone but the government and the media are adept at refocussing frustration on those with even less of a voice.)

Expect a lot of humour punching down at you but just accept it 'because it's just a joke'.

Learn to combine beans with everything for sustenance.

Expect when you try to better yourself for people in many universities to patronise you and find you impolite because your language is coarser and blunter, or because of your new found social status. Don't change that though – it reminds people that they are better than you. Working class, education and intelligence are not mutually exclusive, although if you keep hitting that 6% cider it might prove difficult.

Get used to everyone from outside of Dublin saying it's a shithole, but if you say anything negative about a town or village outside of

Dublin, you'll be accused of being Dublin-centric. Maybe not in so many words, but if you have a strong Dublin accent, even if you aren't a loud and annoying Dub, you'll feel the need to defend your home.

Get used to people judging your accent, which usually starts changing 4-5 weeks after the other symptoms of turning working class begin, before they listen to what you say. You'll be spoken over. Constantly. Especially if you're a woman.

If you get a medical card or rent allowance, you should consider yourself lucky. Seriously, taxi drivers will talk to you about this shit all the time. So never tell anyone you have either of these things.

If you have mental health issues and are on a shoe string budget, just go for a walk. Seriously you can't afford anything else.

Get used to the expectation in your minimum wage job that you are a 'yes' person and always take up the offer of extra work, even if it is your kid's birthday.

If you do have children be prepared for nothing you do to be good enough. Having a pint? You should be at home. Having a smoke? You should be at home. You shouldn't be working that minimum wage job; you belong at home. Why didn't you keep your legs closed until you could afford it?

Expect to be left behind. Your friends with 'good' jobs who did everything sensibly will move on, go on holidays and do all the cool things you wish you could be doing. Some of them will travel poor countries and 'find themselves'. This is a reality for you now though, although perhaps not as extreme. Unfortunately, 70% of your income goes on rent and you don't particularly have any sellable skills so you won't be able to keep up with them and as they become more and more middle class you will fade into obscurity. You would be better off with leprosy than being working class.

Consider sex work as an extra income but then factor in the stigma of being found out and the safety and then go back to eating dry crackers.

If you are made homeless expect people to judge you, want your kids taken off you and comment with statements such as 'why can't you stay with family?' People will know your situation better with minimal details than you know yourself. Being vulnerable automatically means you're a bad person or stupid.

Perhaps you'll stay in an abusive relationship because you can't afford to leave but when you finally do people will bluntly say 'sure, nobody forced you to stay.' I mean Jesus. WHY DIDN'T YOU THINK OF THAT?!

Around the two-month mark of being diagnosed with working-classism you will start to get followed around shops because the symptoms become visible to others.

Expect unsolicited advice on all fronts about how to deal with landlords, how you should spend your money, how you should be saving and watch, just watch, when people judge you for treating yourself to a takeaway. Expect people to speak on your behalf because they expect you to be vulnerable and naïve. Even when you quote big sections from the PRTB to your landlord to get your deposit back.

Walk away from house viewings if there are more than 10 people in the queue. Unless, you've an amazing job you probably won't get it. Don't even try if you're getting rent allowance.

Learn to adapt to fuck all sleep. Be it a combination of stress, poor diet due to fuck all time and money, or just having to do crazy things – you've asked for this.

If you have any allergies, fake or not, forget about them. You're poor now so you can't afford soy products or gluten free bollox.

You will also need to put your clarinet on Ebay and start making your own hummus.

[rEdAcTeD]

There's a hole in the wall behind the door,

And I'm thinking that there's some deep poetic analogy in there,

while I'm fixing it with gauze and mentally listing the other things that I need to mend.

Seriously,

there's something in this;

hoovering all the skin out of the carpet,

washing all the stains off the sheets,

sweeping up the broken mirror shards hidden in the corners,

throwing out every single gift,

erasing photos.

When that wall is sanded over,

it'll be like nothing ever happened.

But I can't make the connection,

because I'm shit at poetry,

so what the fuck would I know?

'hE's My VeRy OwN ChRiStIaN gReY pOpSiClE': rOmAnCe Is DeAd.

We have all to some degree been conditioned to believe in some idea of romance. This is wrong and creates impossible expectations. Well, maybe some people (I'm sure) like to do or be the object all the clichéd stuff like flowers, wedding proposals in a public place, sex on a white bed covered in rose petals, singing people songs written specifically for them on a plane and the idea of a 'prince charming' sweeping you off your feet yada yada yada. I think all of those things are gross and wrong and if anyone expects them they're probably a fool. If someone does any of these things I think it makes them an even bigger fool with no original ideas as to how to show they care about someone. This makes me feel so ill that I can't hide the fact that I feel like this (you can see this from my very obvious and judgemental facial expressions) when people talk about any of these contrived bullshitty things that don't mean anything in the long run. The idea of someone giving me flowers or doing something equally as embarrassing makes me literally want to vomit and this isn't even my main issue with the concept of 'romance'.

My main issue is that the concept of 'romance' is so far removed from reality (albeit my reality) that books like *50 Shades of Grey* are seen as both erotic and romantic. In fact, *50 Shades of Grey* can suck my proverbials for its contrived aspirations, creating a monster so shit that it dried me up within a few pages. With cracking quotes like 'he's my very own Christian Grey popsicle' and "see how you taste," he breathes against my ear. "Suck me, baby (I have massive issues with the use of the word 'baby' unless in an ironic way)" I think the fact that this book became a best seller is indicative of the fact that's there's no such thing as romance anymore, or perhaps the bar is set ridiculously low. It's all just a cringey prelude to sex with the emotional depth of a teaspoon. Now, there's nothing wrong with erotic literature, I'm not saying that, and I'm not saying it needs to be all about riding someone that you're emotionally connected to, but the superficiality of this novel does nothing for me. You can write sex in fiction all you want but there needs to be something more to it – either pure filth or some type of romance, but not both and neither at the same time. Maybe I prefer the tension literature and film as opposed to the actual sex itself, but if the former element has been done correctly the second (although at times superfluous) works out better. The combination of a terrible narrative, crappy BDSM (not the proper good type), awful characters and non-existent romance thrown in together just does not work for me. I don't even know how it works for anyone. It's drawn out and at times painful but that's what makes it work.

Anyway, the reason I am writing about this is because the other night when I was out a man bit my arm repeatedly. 'Was he mad?' I hear you ask. I believe, and I could be wrong here, that this was an attempt on the man's part to win favour with me, and whilst I like biting and all that, I was quite surprised that he took to this course of action whilst I was mid-sentence. Needless to say, this experience left me so perplexed and confused as to what it meant that I thought about it for some time after. Is that what we do now? Is that how we pick people up? That or grind off people on a dance-floor and wake up 5 years later married to someone you don't really know and maybe just settled for? Is there any point in trying to get to know people any more or is it all just a prelude to a ride? I think our expectations as regards finding partners, or even a friend with benefits, deliberately or otherwise, have reached an all- time low. There's no tension. All the barriers have dropped. It's all become very boring and it makes me angry. Even if it's only for a night where's the effort, on anyone's part? Nobody really bothers any more. It's all instant gratification and making the best of a badly chosen situation, riding someone you just met in the jacks who's snorting cocaine off your tits.

Dick pics, sexting, Snap Chat fingerings. It's all grand but every time I'm single, because I'm out of a long-term thing, everything has changed so much and the expectations are even lower. I mean I'm not shaming anyone who does these things but all this stuff moves along so quickly that I nearly feel like I'm suffering from something that makes my brain majorly confused. It makes me feel old… But then again, what would I know about romance considering the amount of difficulty I have expressing positive emotions anyway?

TiPs On HoW tO nOt BuRsT iNtO cOmPlEte FlAmEs

1: Not everyone feels the same way you do about things – we're all different – so don't assume that everyone will have the same priorities as you.

2: If you're bursting for a wee walk in backwards to the bathroom and open your trousers before you even look at the toilet to avoid your bladder getting excited and pissing yourself.

3: Ask yourself questions before making a negative comment: What's the point in saying this? Is there a positive suggestion to rectify the situation accompanying this statement? What is there to gain by saying this?

4: There is no point in fighting on the internet. Keep away from comment sections.

5: Compartmentalise every element of your life so if one part goes on fire that the whole thing doesn't explode.

6: Don't waste your time hating people. Complete waste of energy.

7: Looking back at past events can be helpful to avoid repetition. However, if you look back too much you won't go anywhere else.

8: If you get a sweaty bum when sitting on a glossy surface before standing wipe your bum along the surface to remove the sweat shape of your arse.

9: Belly buttons are useful for storing shower gel when in the bath.

10: Instrumental music is a good background for creativity.

11: Getting up early is the only way to be productive.

12: You can't give 100%, 100% of time. Aim for 50%, 75% of the time.

13: If you have to get up early but you're locked go asleep somewhere really uncomfortable so you wake up before your alarm.

14: Invest – at least equally – if not more, in platonic friendships – not romantic ones. You can get everything you need without being in a relationship, with lots of friends and sex toys.

15: Seriously, stop trying to rap. You've been doing this in private for years. You really can't do it Caroline – get over it.

16: If you want to learn how to 'network' forget that fucking word and just try to make genuine human connections.

17: Accept that some people don't really know or understand you – and that's fine – they don't deserve that anyway.

18: Do not take kitchen knives out of their packaging and put them back in your backpack.

19: It's better to want things than to need them. Other than essentials like food and shelter you don't really need anything.

20: Social media can get you the ride if you play your cards right.

21: If you have heartburn in bed sleep on your left hand side.

22: Kegels are super important and do improve sex. They make your vag magic if you do them right.

23: Hug and cuddle people. Share beds with platonic friends and spoon. It's lovely and releases oxytocin and makes ya happy and calm.

24: Laugh at people's shite jokes – particularly men – they love that. Fragile dopes.

25: Disappear sometimes and don't tell anyone where you are. Turn your phone off and all.

26: Being angry makes you more productive than being sad. If you work this out sooner rather than later you can turn loads of things around.

27: Constantly examine patterns in your life and if the same problems keep happening change that shit up.

28: If you're feeling broody offer to babysit a child with colic. That'll fix ya.

29: I don't know if it's just me but my period has gone nuts since I hit my thirties. If you're like me for the first two days of the 'red army' hide away from anyone you may be likely to punch.

30: Eyebrows frame your face – have good eyebrows.

31: If someone touches someone from the waist down they probably fancy them.

32: Positivity is more productive than negativity, and in many cases, on a individual level, more conducive to eliciting a positive response or change.

33: If you fancy someone avoid them like the plague, unless you're super drunk. You'll just say something stupid anyway. At least you'll have the excuse you were drunk.

34: Dick is abundant and of low value.

35: If attempting to pleasure a woman consistency of motion is very important. Don't change things up just before she pops. I'm not a man so I don't care about whether it's the same for you.

36: Reply to annoying messages with random facts about Skeletor or some rare parrot.

37: Expectations can ruin things so generally have none – just basics that need to be met.

38: Fear engulfment that comes with relationships. Maintain your own individuality and never expose vulnerabilities.

39: Bring up issues as soon as you can but when you feel you have processed enough emotionally to be rational.

40: Try to avoid raising your voice. Scream into a pillow later or have an angry wank later.

41: Never call a woman 'loud', 'irrational', 'stupid', 'pig' or 'emotional' without expecting negative backlash you asshole. Never say she is 'overreacting' unless you want to see what overreacting actually looks like.

42: Sometimes people just want to vent – not for you to fix anything. If you don't know what to say just actively listen.

43: Ask people questions about themselves to get to know them. I know this sounds obvious but there is literally no way of really getting to know someone without asking them things. It also shows you are interested in them.

44: Keep your coffee grounds in the fridge.

45: Always carry baby wipes. You'll be grateful for them if there's no jacks roll.

46: Toss a coin to make decisions like 'who should I bring home tonight?' or 'should I leave my job?'

47: Let kitties come to you.

48: Show people how to make you happy in bed and if they react badly that's their business.

49: People project onto each other loads. Listen to them. It's not you, it's them.

50: Avoid people who say all their ex-partners were crazy. The only common denominator there is them, innit?

If My Cv WeRe TrUe

28/06/19

To whom it may concern,

I am only applying for this job in the hopes that you turn me down because I just want to tell people that I have been looking for 'gainful employment.'

I would much rather gouge my own eyes than work for you, but, if you decide I 'have what it takes' I can promise you that I work moderately hard for you for the first few moths until I inevitably get bored and leave. I won't thank you for minimum wage and obviously resent being micromanaged to the point that you won't talk to me any more. I dislike authority in any shape or form and in time you will learn this.

I have terrible communication skills due to actually being a nervous introvert who unfortunately gets pegged as an extrovert due to her drinking problem. I am incapable of small talk.

Positives include that I probably won't ride anyone in the office, or at least you won't find out about it. I learned that lesson last time,

AMIRITE?! I think my greatest accomplishment, though, is preventing others from being productive around me. If you want to have races on the office chairs down ramps or see how many pegs employees can fit on their face during working hours – I am your woman!

Please find my CV attached,

Kind regards,

Caroline Egan

Caroline Egan

Some stupid email I had since college.com
Some completely overpriced bedsit

KEY SKILLS

Technical Skills

I am proficient in editing, correcting grammar and syntax.

I am a regular user of online resources such as Wordpress, Facebook, Twitter, Quora and Instagram, (so you will find me on social media a lot instead of working)

I have a proven track record in meeting deadlines – no matter how tight.

Conflict resolution – between intoxicated people.

Have learned strong digital marketing skills with Facebook, Adwords etc.

Video and audio production and editing.

Decent memory for song lyrics, with a specific interest in 1995-2000.

I have a strong academic background.

Taking selfies that make me look attractive

Looking after adult children.

Certificate in photography.

Personal Skills

I have a strong network of contacts in arts, culture and music.

Believable fake listening.

I have a very strong insider knowledge of Dublin through personal experience.

Shutting down emotionally like a robot when distressed.

Flexibility and straight forward, honest communication.

Pretending I don't have mental health issues.

I am willing and open to create content about subjects that I am unfamiliar with.

Going out the night before and STILL going into work.

Running away from problems.

Pretending that I'm thick so I won't have to do things.

Accumulating useless skills.

EDUCATION

I have coasted this far in life, as I have a good memory and am clever enough. As a result, I spent 12 years in college accumulating these useless skill before dropping out from a PhD due to bit of a 'breakdown.'

EMPLOYMENT

Freelance Journalist

I took this job because I wanted to sit alone at home in my pjs and smoke and masturbate whenever I want. I do my work, but I'm on my own. This suits me better.

English Tutor

I taught students Post-Colonial Theory, Non-Realist Fiction and Popular Literature. I was completely out of my depth, and although I enjoyed slagging off students, I suffered from extreme imposter syndrome .

Radio Presenter/researcher

I did this thankless job for several months on a show that was essentially the Joe Duffy show on local issues. This was an internship but despite doing 90% of the work I got zero credit. I left because of this and the uncomfortable sexual attitude of the older men in the office.

TV and Video Production Lecturer

I had to try to get a pack of stoners to make videos. Many were the same age as me. You can guess how that went.

Film Reviewer

I reviewed films and sometimes albums. I received lots of free things. It was good but unpaid so really was fucking pointless.

Hobbies

Writing poor erotic fiction
Making tiny engine sounds with my mouth
Drawing dicks on things.
Defacing things with googly eyes

Playing hide and seek
Looking after drunk people
Late night phone calls
Thumb wrestling
Drinking pints in one go
Rapping in secret
Crying at robot related things.

References

Please give me warning so I can get my friends to pretend to be former bosses.

wOrDs AnD pHrAsEs ThAt ShOuLd ExIsT, iF tHeY dOn'T aLrEaDy.

Here is a list of words and phrases that I think should be used if they aren't already:

'Mind deaf'

When you cannot hear your own thoughts because someone is talking too much – usually a child or drunk person.

'My head was wrecked because he just wouldn't shut up. I went completely mind deaf.'

'Dipster'

An accidental older hipster, who doesn't think they're a hipster but they totally look like one and are kinda a dick.

'Did you see him vaping outside the vegan restaurant talking about wind energy?'

'What a dipster.'

'Trench cunt'

Similar to 'trench foot', but obviously with a vagina. When the area starts to go all weird from being too wet and goes all crinkley like you spent too long in the bath. Very likely to lead to a urinary tract infection – so make sure you pee!

'I can't get comfortable today after all the bangs yesterday – I think I have trench cunt.'

'Bastard'

A person who sits on the outside of the seat on a bus and/or has their bag still up on the seat when the bus is packed.

'There were loads of bastards on the bus today and I couldn't get a seat.'

'Interferon'

A person who likes to interfere with whatever you are doing because they seem to think you can't do anything correctly.

'He kept coming in and trying to stir my shit when I was in the kitchen. Fucking interferon.'

'Old fashioned.'

A role play involving the man coming home drunk, shouting at his partner to get back in the kitchen, holding a picture of the Pope and taking his belt off to give her a good auld beating.

'Ah man, I'm in bits today because I had an old fashioned last night.'

'Deja vag'

The moment when you walk into a situation and notice that multiple of your past partners or people you've slept with (also known as the collective 'an awkward of exs') are all around each other and talking.

You don't know if they know about each other and you don't like it or what they could be talking about. You don't like it one bit.

'I got total deja vag last night and it feels like I heard the word anal mentioned. I'm fucking mortified.'

'Blackout bleeeeernds.'

This should just simply replace the normal noun of blackout blinds purely because it makes me laugh. I burped trying to say blackout blinds before and it came out like this. Now I can only say 'blackout bleeeeernds.' No example needed.

'Prawn'

Use this word to deliberately infuriate a 14-year-old whilst playing chess with him, pretending you are thick, instead of the correct phrase 'pawn.'

'So the prawn can only move one space yeah?'

'IT'S CALLED A PAWN MOTHER YOU FUCKING IDIOT!'

'And the prawn can only move forward too yeah?'

'INAUDIBLE ANGRY GIBBERISH.'

'Shakespearing.'

When someone is super locko and going off on a diatribe that nobody either gets or is listening to. Much like a monologue in Shakespearean plays.

'He was pretty drunk. He was all Shakespearing about the Celtic tiger and the crash… I think.'

'Jambon Jovi.'

A cool name for a jambon.

'Jammie dodger.'

Someone who won't have sex with someone when they have their period.

'I have such a horn on me but the red army has come to visit.'

'Oh is he a jammie dodger?'

(Insert sad face here)

'Amusement park'

A person you would ride continuously for the weekend but never again. Possibly involving pre-emptive purchase of the morning after pill.

'They're not really relationship material to be honest. And that's not what I was looking for anyway but they are a decent amusement park.'

'Hangover horn'

I'm pretty sure people use this but had to explain this concept to someone recently. Upon awakening after an excessive night of drinking, filled with fear and a headache, there is a massive rise in vulnerability and libido. This sometimes results in a worsening of the symptoms of the hangover but is an urge that is very hard to resist.

'I had the worst hangover horn ever this morning. After I had that bang I puked.'

'Ghost whispering'

When you hear someone say the exact thing you said as if it was their idea in the first place.

'That motherfucking prick is passing my idea off as his own about my podcast! What am I? The fucking ghost whisperer?'

'Dissing'

When someone messages you that you don't like and you pretend you got a new phone in the hopes that they'll get the message.

'U STILL UP? WANT TO HAVE SUM FUN?'

'NEW PHONE. WHO DIS?'

'YoUr DaDdY wAs A mOtHeRfUcKeR': sEx TaLkS wItH yOuR kIdS

'Bukkake is when multiple men love one woman and…'

Hahaha … nah – that's not how it went down I apparently did explain it to my chisler before but not like that. Just so you know it was because it came up on a card in Cards Against Humanity and in the interest of honesty and openness I felt the need to tell him in a no-frills way what that meant.

So how did I get to the point where I don't get embarrassed by sex talk with the kid? I feel like this is next level openness that would make a lot of people squirm. I mean, I feel, it's really important to be completely transparent with the kid, so that he isn't scared of anything or awkward or ashamed or anything, and I also wanted to make sure that I never interrupt him or have to deal with the aftermath of said enjoyment. It's got to the point where I screamed at him not to go into a certain drawer in my room and he laughed saying 'are there condoms in there?' to which I sheepishly lied 'yes', despite the fact that I had hidden something way more sinister of a sexual nature in the drawer.

Ok firstly, have you met me? If you have you know I'm a frigging open book and could potentially talk about sex stuff all day. Thing is, I remember being traumatised by the conversation that I had about the birds and the bees with my mam. I must have been like seven or something and had heard a woman give out to her son on some soap because he had 'got someone pregnant'. I followed my mam around for like two days constantly asking 'how did he get her pregnant?' and she fobbed me off as best she could. But I was intrigued and relentless and finally, she gave up and explained. SO after the basic facts were explained to me, and it seemed like a massive big deal, with a dropped jaw I asked if it hurt (because it totally sounded like that whichever way she explained it). To which she replied with a gross little chuckle that still disturbs me 'no'. For days I couldn't look at men. I wouldn't want that shit with my kid.

When he was tiny, about five or six, I decided to get it over with. Sitting in the park I quickly explained the whole thing, thinking it would easier to get it over with sooner (and not make it sound like it fricking hurt). 'Any questions?' I said somewhat apathetically afterwards and he said 'nope' and then we went to get ice cream. I had contemplated if it went badly to just throw that Santa wasn't real into the mix to throw the focus off the sex part – but it didn't come to that thank fuck. From there I made jokes about how he was conceived as the result of a terrible boating accident (it's an elaborate story involving a bath and shame) but it made everything kind of funny and I could see after a while that the whole sex issue wasn't a big deal to him.

Two years later and he's accidentally seen a porn pop up of a lady giving some dude a blowie and because of our close relationship, I was able to wheedle that he had in fact seen it out of him. Now, I'm not anti-porn by any stretch, and I know it's a fact of life that he was going to come across it. I have some issues with certain things but overall it's just a thing that's there. I just really wanted to make sure that he wasn't mixing up fantasy and reality because this was so young and maybe it would skew his expectations of real life. Porn wasn't really a thing for me at all until I had been out riding at least six years so I wondered about the proliferation of porn and how that could have an impact on someone seeing it way before they would ever see another naked person in real life. 'It's so unnatural – why would anyone want to put a willy in a mouth?' he asked. My reply was quick and to the point and something along the lines of 'look it's what happens sometimes. You'll probably want that when you're older. There's nothing really wrong with it but you're way too young to have seen that. Also, that really isn't like real life – people have way more hair on their bits.' And that was that.

I wanted to remove the awkwardness and shame from the whole thing so that he wouldn't end up having some kind of weird complex, but I didn't want him frightened of it either. I've told him it's natural to be curious but that all this isn't real life. I've tried to make it as light-hearted as possible so that if he needs me that he'll ask for me for things. I obviously want him to have his privacy but once the cards are on the table the stigma is removed. We're probably freakishly close and open and it might make people uncomfortable but I think it's healthy enough like?

One tip though when talking to your kid that I would 100% advise is to not bring personal experience into it. It brings the cringe factor in big time and to be honest it's TMI even for me. I remember going to the doctor when I was 16, asking for the morning after pill back when it was a bitch to get, (and also asking and being refused the normal pill but that's another story) and telling the doctor that the condom split and he said 'I hate it when that happens.' And he was old and gross and I didn't and still don't want to picture that weird little man having sex.

'Seriously you need to be careful when you start having sex, OK?' I said. 'You're not at it now are ya?'

'Don't worry mam, I won't get anyone up the duff' he said smugly.

And then we laughed. Oh how we laughed.

Am I doing this right? Fucked if I know.

THiS wOmAn WrOtE aBoUt VaGiNaS ONlInE – WhAt HaPpEnEd NeXt WiLl ShOcK yOu

I have a love/hate relationship with the internet. I think maybe most of us do. Thoughts that we would've let go into the ether can be shared with all the people that we deem loosely to be 'friends' on the internet. On nights out when I have the app installed on my phone I have to make sure that my statuses are made available to 'only me' in case I decide to write something drunk that makes no sense. This happens more often than I'd care to admit.

I think the positives, (before I get into them) far outweigh the negative aspects of social media, however. You can talk to your friends in Japan, share events and use it for publicity for your own little self-indulgent blog, share ideas and have a nice open exchange of ideas (although this is getting rarer). You can reconnect with people that you have no seen in years and continue your friendship from where you left off. You can feel that you are in some way included in people's everyday lives and see what that kid that you will never go to see looks like. You can see what people are doing on their holidays and you can get an idea on peoples' political views. In many ways, the online persona, can add a bit of depth to your character, or at least present viewpoints that you weren't aware that they held before, or a hobby that you never knew they had. You can go to specific groups, secret or otherwise, for a whole range of support, education and motivation. You can look for jobs, make videos for people who are abroad, or far away, on their birthdays or just communicate for free with friends when you've run out of credit. The positive possibilities are endless.

Despite this there is a ridiculous number of contemporary artists out there painting pictures of hordes of zombies staring down at their phones or in some pseudo pretentious way trying to show that girls' self-esteem is based on the amount of 'likes' a selfie gets. The bang of self-righteousness off them is unreal, coupled with the fact that not only are these unoriginal ideas, but also the irony that these images are shared on social media itself. Fuck that noise!

In the past, social media has made me paranoid about relationships – rightfully so, as well, because people aren't even stupid enough to cover their tracks properly. It has also shown me that I am gradually growing apart from older friendships as they go on nights out without me, or have pictures of themselves up at events where I was never invited. That's not to say that I'm bitter or anything but in many ways, it's concrete proof, visual confirmation, of what you already know. That clearly doesn't make it easier to swallow. In many ways, the ability to sleuth around on the internet and spy on people you are no longer connected to makes it more difficult to get over things – because there you go, clicking on pages, reopening old wounds, or seeing some arsehole you used to know doing well at life. I mean, there is a certain amount to relish, when you see the opposite as well, and that person you dislike isn't doing well, and maybe that's what you were hoping to find on their Facebook page anyway. People you were meant to drift away from are still always there in the background, reminding you of the life they are living that you are no longer a part of and you have to wonder, whether still 'friends' online with them or not whether this is actually healthy. Sometimes, coupled with 'friends' successes you might feel left behind, not only by them, but because your life sucks in comparison. Perhaps, I'm an over-sharer, but fuck it; I'm sure most of us have felt like this at some point, even if you only rarely log in.

I can understand that people perhaps think I am constantly on the internet with nothing better to do, but considering most of my time is spent in front of computer, either for work or pleasure (in every way that you could interpret that), it shouldn't really surprise people that I am here. I often hear people talk about people saying 'oh they post too much' and admittedly I've thought that too, because if I'm honest I don't care about pictures of dogs, or your lunch, but still I never really judge about it. If I don't like someone's posts I don't follow them. Simple as. And I don't make a judgement about a person based on things as arbitrary as whether they love their dog or are super enthusiastic about sharing music videos – I judge them on their opinions and their treatment of other people. I personally have quite often felt that I have been having a one-way conversation with people in real life, where people just go on rants in my direction, never ask me questions or actually listen anyway so over the years of using Facebook I began to gradually subconsciously use it as a platform to converse, because I was sick of people making assumptions about me without them ever actually hearing the words I was saying, which also contributed to the blog, and eventually this book, becoming a thing. It's not that I think that I have anything very unusual or interesting to say, but it's nice to leave the ideas hanging out there, and potentially show people other aspects to my personality, other than the woman half locked singing Charles and Eddie in the pub on a Friday night.

One thing I don't understand, and probably will never get right, is the collecting of 'friends'. Now I'm well aware that many people have vast numbers of 'friends' because they have travelled, or work in a certain industry that requires networking, but to be honest how does anyone have more than 1,000 people on their list? I'm not being a dick, but seriously… To be honest, it screams to me of a creepy dude, just adding randos so he can request nudes, throwing out friend requests to attractive girls that he may have said 'hello' to once. It's quality not quantity dudes – not fucking Pokémon. I suppose it depends on the level of information that you share online as well, but personally I would not feel comfortable with more than 500 friends on my page at any time and I regularly clear them out, because if I'm being realistic here, do I really even know 500 people? And I like to share things, not to be an edgelord or controversial, but to potentially make people laugh or present a different perspective. I think my online persona is actually a pretty accurate representation of who I am, and it's not something I could be arsed sharing with everyone. I'm more confident and articulate online than in real life I'm shyer and overwhelmed with anxiety a lot of the time, but these still are my thoughts, percolated and condensed, in an easy- to-read version of my busy busy brain and perhaps, not everyone deserves to see this. Some of my 'friends' I have never met in real life, like my American pen pal or some lovely ladies that I'm friends with from groups, but I keep them because we interact and I find their posts engaging, and these are all part of a network of people that have helped me form my own opinions and live perfectly well without leaving the house.

I've been deleted in the past, as we all have, but I really don't know whether or not I should, unless someone ignores me in the street or actively pisses me off in real life. I remember the time, on my business page, that I made a joke about selfie sticks and vaginas, and all hell broke loose. You'd swear people never heard the word before, let alone from a girl and a few people were up-in-arms about my vulgar choice of humour. I was called a slut, had horrible memes put on my page saying 'your parents must be very proud' and men in my life were called on by conservative women to 'talk some sense into me' because it was so 'unladylike.' Personally, I thought the joke was hilarious, did a lot of banning on my Facebook writing page and tutted, but I know it caused people to delete me. Your own level of what is appropriate or not is up to you, but I'm not hurting anyone or being mean, and there's no one way that a girl, particularly one who doesn't care what some rando thinks as to what constitutes what a woman should say, think or do, so scroll on if you hate it because I'm not going to stop writing and posting and doing my thing, regardless of your superficial online confidence to tear people (particularly women) down online.

[cLiCkS fInGeRs]

Do you

think

if I

hit

enter

enough it

will

look

like

it means

something

profound?

hOw To StOp FeElInG lIkE sHiT bEcAuSe YoU'rE a WoRtHlEsS uGlY wOmAn

We all know that our looks are where most of our worth comes from right? And maybe recently you've just come to the conclusion that you mightn't be even average looking because somebody told you that you were an ugly bitch. Look, it's not your fault OK? You were born with deficient genes and that whole myth of 'marry a rich man' that your mother sold you instead of cultivating a rich sense of independence and pride in your own interests and work ethic is kinda fucked now isn't it? If you had just realised that you were ugly sooner. Goddammit.

Here are some tips to better your situation because if you want to bag a man you're going to have to put in waaaay more effort than an ugly man was. TO achieve your destiny of being looked after by mediocre man, bound in contract by marriage, you really need to be good looking BUT there are a few things that you can do to improve your situation so you don't need to start your collection of spinster cats just yet. We all know there is no way you can be happy on your own, so the first element in order to salvage anything is to just accept the cold hard reality – you are an ugly bitch.

So what do you do, eh? Well here's what I've done. Hopefully it works for you, but my results aren't in yet. Maybe it took me too long to realise that I was bet with the ugly stick because I was distracted with child rearing and college, but there is hope for you and hopefully we won't all rot on the shelves, bemoaning a lack of average dick in our lives.

1: Buy women's magazines constantly. There's nothing like a load of people tearing women down for their body changes or dress choices to make you feel even slightly better about yourself. Also, it can have the flip-side effect of upsetting you more, because despite their body changes, especially after having a baby, they still look better than you and this will motivate you to improve that sack of shit of a body of yours.

2: You can trick men online and lure them in by using filters on your social media selfies. Want giant eyes or dog ears? Those gullible guys will be believing it no bother. Show a bit of tit to get a bit of sausage in your inbox and requests to show 'bobs and vagine' from enthusiastic foreign men.

3: Use copious amounts of concealer. Concealer is amazing. It covers blemishes, redness, your puffy eyes from crying all night because you're lonely… When used correctly it even covers all definable features. That's right – cover up every inch of your ugly face with concealer so that you are indistinguishable from your former self. It's better to be a blank expressionless slate than have a horrible face – which you do.

4: As part of accepting that you are worthless and ugly, ensure that you take all criticisms on board. Random men will tell you how you're ugly so just politely listen to their suggestions, no matter how hypocritical it may appear or how you didn't ask in the first place. They are doing you a favour. Do not and I repeat, do not, get angry with them as there is absolutely nothing more unattractive than an angry ugly woman – who is probably some kind of feminazi or something. You'll never get a dicking acting like that.

5: If all your clothing is as bad as your face and body you should set it on fire and just wear bin bags.

6: Work on your personality – now, I know you didn't want it to come to this, but you really should consider it. No longer will you be an empty receptacle waiting for men to come and fill you with their thoughts, ideas and ejaculate. Now, I'm not saying be clever – because if The Big Bang Theory has taught me anything – it's that the more intelligent a woman is the less physically attractive she is, but also men are intimidated by those rare few women that have bigger brains than them. Instead, try (and the emphasis is on 'try' here as science has shown that women aren't as funny as men) to be funny. Use this as a last resort, obviously, but there are quite a few relatively funny unattractive women who have used this to their advantage.

7: Accept that you are chubby because you are lazy and eat too much. It definitely doesn't have anything to do with having had a kid, loose skin, PCOS or that drinking problem that started because you had a bit of a mental breakdown. Nope, it's cos you eat like a bastard. Anyone calling you obese knows that. Remember even if you did love yourself and your body, in all your chubby glory, it's wrong because you're clearly actively promoting an unhealthy lifestyle choice.

8: Women aren't meant to be hairy either FFS. Despite the fact that hair grows pretty much in all the same places as men have hair it's gross for us to have it. It has nothing to do with an attempt during World War II to generate more income for razors by opening up a new market towards women. Nada. Your natural body hair is gross and you should be ashamed. Seriously remove it or do you want to start collecting dust in your vagina now?

9: I think your standards as an ugly lady may have been too high? I mean have you been single long like? What about that guy that's been messaging you every day for the last year sending dick pics?

He seems OK when you put it in perspective right? Why don't you give him a chance before you dry up? Lower those standards – even if you have nothing in common with those unattractive guys, cos let's face it you've a face like an 80-year-old ballsack.

10: If you have big tits get them out as much as you can, in a good bra to take the focus away from that trainwreck of a face. This can even distract from your fatness too.

11: Smile – smile constantly and manically. There is nothing worse than a sad/angry ugly woman. I mean what you, a feminist? Remember men constantly telling you to 'cheer it up, it might never happen', despite your dog dying earlier that day? They're telling you how looking at you is upsetting them. How could you be so selfish?

12: If all else fails send nudes. Nobody looks at the mantelpiece when they're poking the fire. Just make sure your ugly mantelpiece isn't in it and that the fire is at a flattering angle.

Good luck you ugly bastards.

25 WaYs To DeFiNiTeLy PuLI WoMeN sInCe EvErYtHiNg HaS bEeN rUiNeD fOr MeN

Sure ya can't even look at women now, can ya? All this #metoo stuff has gone too far and sure now ya can't even approach a woman. Well I'm here to offer some helpful advice – advice that I feel I can freely offer as a woman and a woman who likes men and women. So get out your notebook and in no time at all you'll have women frothing at the gash for ya.

Tell them you're an alpha male

It's really hard to tell if someone is an alpha male. Biologically women are drawn towards an alpha male. We spot them through status symbols such as fancy watches and clothes and also by the less subtle 'I'm an alpha male' dropped into conversation. Seriously, if you have nothing else going for you apart from money you'll be grand but we won't always know unless you boast. You are a predator. An apex predator made to dominate.

Offer them opportunities to better themselves by negging.

Not only does the backhanded compliment show that you're paying attention and hoping for them to improve themselves, it misdirects women away from your own insecurities. Got a micro penis? Have less of a personality than a sack of spuds? It's OK if you tell her she'd be good looking if she lost some weight. She's lucky you chose to talk to her. Seriously, she'll appreciate it.

Talk about how much you enjoy giving pleasure to a woman.

You'd think this is the baseline for a good sexual experience but it isn't. Tell her about how important it is to you even if you haven't a fucking clue what to do to a woman once you get one. You are a fucking unicorn.

If they talk to you they like you.

If a woman talks to you for more than 5 minutes she is more than likely into you. Fact.

Wear them down.

When they show disinterest they are just playing hard to get. Women generally don't know what they want till you show them. How many romantic comedies have revolved around men showing how much they care by continuously trying to win them over. Fight for them. And keep fighting them till they get tired enough to give up. Sometimes they need to just lower their standards and not be so stuck up, am I right?

Explain how women are to them.

You can explain how women are objectively to them and women will take that on board completely. Make massive generalisations about women because they're all the same and too stupid to realise it. So, what if you only know your mother and your cousin? Objectivity is the key.

Tell them how they're not like other girls.

Women are shit to each other and men. Putting other women down makes the woman you're talking to feel great. Of course, they want to be seen as different to ALL other women. They are special. And therefore of more value to men.

Nothing gets me wetter than someone talking about how great Jordan Peterson is to me.

I love him. Bring up all his conservative pseudo-science to really hammer home how men should be in charge. I mean his is a science guy, isn't he?

Ask them a question and then talk over them anyway.

Sure you know what they are going to answer anyway.

Don't hide your wedding ring.

Women love honest men.

If they have their boobs, legs or whatever on display – they are totally up for it.

This is a good way to select a lady.

If they smile at you, you are in there.

Even if you've kinda cornered them and they can't escape and are trying to be polite.

Compliment their tits.

They love that. They're usually super unaware of how big or firm they are.

Women need men's guidance.

Have they a PhD in something? You probably still know more. You should tell them everything you know. That'll impress them.

Be loud and show off.

It shows your youthful side. Women love big children.

If things aren't going your way start a fight with one of your friends to prove how masculine you are. Women love the smell of misplaced testosterone.

Bring a guitar to a party and play songs like Wonderwall so loud that everyone has to look at you.

Talk about travelling and how it changed you.

They're not drinking?

How are they going to loosen up for you to get in? Keep at them till they drink. Put extra smoke in their joints until they can't see properly. They'll start finding you attractive, probably open their legs for ya and even if they claim they didn't consent there will be fuck all repercussions for you anyway – especially if you have rich parents.

Ask them to show you where the toilets are.

Then jump them. Girls love the element of surprise.

The classic never-failing mating call of the female is dancing.

This is pretty much an invitation to rub your willy off them. Do it.

Demonstrate your value by bringing your sad ex out with you who still has feelings for you. Everyone will notice her sad face when you talk to other attractive women, making you look cool, and if the worst happens, you can ride her later and then 'regret' it the following day.

Money

Women just want your money. Casually open a filled wallet, talk about rich your Dad is and buy yourself expensive drinks to give us an instant horn. Money is more important than style or substance to us.

Women aren't funny but laugh almost hysterically at their jokes.

Hit them in the feelz about a broken heart.

If all else fails try and get a sympathy shag by talking about how your life has been horrible.

Slag beta males off in front of females.

This will impress them no end, even if they are their friends. Even if they are mid conversation. You are an alpha. You are entitled to their attention and company!

DoWnLoAdInG aN aBoRtIoN

The cat sat in front of me, her eyes locked on mine. She mewled, and when I failed to respond to her calls because of searing cramps and tears, she slunk closer winding her tail around my legs, before springing up beside me on the couch. I stretched out on my back slowly, inhaling and exhaling sharply, every contraction with a sharper edge my boyfriend's arms wrapping. I held the remnants of the first tablet under my tongue, foaming slightly at the mouth, terrified to swallow them. I sat awkwardly, in pain, the focus of everyone's attention in the room. I knew that the bleeding was starting, and soon had to run to the bathroom to vomit, followed by the meowing cat.

It isn't really a choice if you have no other options available to you. I knew this when I stood frozen, staring at the blue lines on the urine-splashed test for what could've been an hour, I don't remember, blank and sick at the same time. I knew this when I glanced around my lousy overpriced little flat. I knew this when I saw my boyfriend's face when I showed him the positive result on the pregnancy test. I knew this when I considered working, on my own, while pregnant in my minimum-wage job and the physical impossibilities of maintaining the low standard of living that I had grown accustomed to. I knew I had nothing to offer a child, right now. The alternatives were also pretty bleak; raising a huge amount of money to travel to England only to return, bleeding on a plane, or to illegally buy and import tablets, which were unreliable, and if I were caught, could earn me 14 years in prison.

As I wretched and heaved into the sink, in the tiny damp bathroom, the cat seemed worried. She weaved between my bare legs and her meows turned to yowls, and when I sat down the toilet to investigate the bleeding, she tried jumping onto my lap until I prevented her with my forearm. My underwear was now soaked and bright red blood streaked my thighs as I forced my pants down. I could feel the sweat building on my face, but at the same time I was cold, shivering, and sore. For a moment I wondered if it wasn't working, or if there were complications, or if I was going into shock. If so, I'd have to go to the hospital, and that sent a wave of anxiety through me. I had no money, lived somewhere terrible and would most likely lose my job if pregnant. That's when I realized this wasn't a choice; it was a necessity. I cried, tears streaking my face as I thought about the possibility of getting arrested despite the fact that if there really were job opportunities, or affordable places to live, I would be happy to be pregnant with a potentially beautiful curly haired child. As I dwelled on how bad of a bad person I was, my boyfriend knocked on the door to see if I was OK, or more likely, to see that I was actually following though with the whole thing.

The process of acquiring the tablets was long and stressful. I had to source an address where I could receive the tablets, and there was a chance it could be intercepted. If that happened, I had no idea of what the repercussions would be beyond remaining pregnant. I went online, after my friend directed me to website where the pills were imported from India. I filled in my details. 'How pregnant are you?' the site asked. Years of irregular periods made this question hard to answer. I made an educated guess of eight weeks, but in hindsight it was probably more likely ten or eleven. The site advised against using the tablets after ten weeks.

How long would they take to arrive? My stomach knotted. If one small part of this whole process went wrong, the consequences could be dire. I was risking my freedom and health, but there was no other way. 'Will you need counselling?' the site asked. I answered 'no' despite the fact that I knew my decision was based on my circumstances, not an actual choice – and that I would always be plagued by the 'what ifs' of continuing the pregnancy. I made a donation to the site, which offered services to women in similar situations. Then, I waited, and felt utterly helpless. I tracked the parcel over the next ten days obsessively each day and made arrangements with work to take three off days, enough time, I hoped to collect the tablets and perform my illegal home abortion.

I lay on the couch wrapped in blankets, my torso on my boyfriend's lap, as he stroked my hair and I sobbed quietly. The pain was unbearable, and I began to think that maybe I was further along than I had guessed. Apparently the further along you are, the more it hurts. I wondered if I would see the fetus, and whether it would be recognizable as the start of a human. All the while, as the pressure increased on my womb and shivering with contractions, I kept reassuring myself that this was the right decision. I just wanted it to be all over.

My boyfriend offered me chocolate and downloaded films for us to watch and I wondered whether he would be able to handle this. He rubbed my back and kissed my forehead and said and did all the right things, but was this simply to ensure that I went through with it? When I had found out that I was pregnant he simply kept repeating the phrase 'I'm not ready' over and over again. There was never any question how I had felt about the whole situation. So it wasn't really a choice for me again. Was what he was doing this because he actually cared or was he just terrified that I would make him a father against his will? As he cracked open a third can all I felt was resentment.

The day that we went to collect the parcel was racked with anxiety from the offset. I woke up stressed and irritated, and when eventually we got the bus for a three-hour journey I was ready to explode. My boyfriend held my hand but had insisted on annoying me by singing stupid songs and telling me to 'cheer up' for the entire journey. I felt that if it were his body that was in trouble, the tune would be different. For most of the journey I tried to ignore the stress and planned how I would take the tablets and the timing involved. The instructions that I had read online read as follows: *take one tablet 24 hours before (mifepristone) and then take two batches of misoprostol at intervals of a few hours apart.*

There was an extra batch of the misoprostol, just in case I thought it didn't work. Under normal circumstances, in countries where abortion is legal, these tablets could be administered vaginally but because abortion was illegal in Ireland the tablets have to be held under the tongue until they dissolve, so if you presented at a hospital saying you are miscarrying they cannot tell if you did so deliberately. All of this filled me with dread. On the bus home to Dublin I took the mifepristone and tried to nap.

Travelling abroad for a proper procedure would have been impossible. It was just too much money, and my morning sickness even made walking to work difficult. Each morning on my walk, I vomited all the way down the street. A plane ride would have out of the question, not to mention the many difficulties that come with undergoing a medical procedure in a foreign country.

Ireland didn't even make exceptions for cases with severe birth defects, so expectant mothers were required by law to carry fetuses to term even if the child was expected to die just after birth, forcing them to endure another loss.

Holding the tablets under my tongue was traumatic. It took approximately 30 minutes for them to dissolve and filter into my system. Foamy drool dripped out the sides of my lips as I struggled to swallow the saliva, but not the tablets. I put on my oldest pyjamas and a giant sanitary towel. I sighed, re-read the instructions and took note of this advice: *If you are experiencing too much pain and bleeding you should go to a hospital,* immediately causing me to wonder how much pain was too much pain. And then there was the question of what I should do next? Should I go to my doctor for a check-up afterwards and pretend I had a miscarriage?

There have been cases of women getting caught taking these tablets. In Northern Ireland, a woman was prosecuted for having an illegal home abortion when her room-mate ratted her out to the authorities. The fear of being found out, or the parcel getting intercepted, added to the trauma of an event that no woman actively wants to endure in the first place. I can guarantee you that nobody wants to have an abortion. No woman wants to have an unnecessary operation, one that is illegal and can be highly expensive. No woman wants to experience pain. It is a measure of last resort, a decision made for financial reasons or because the fetus has birth defects, or because there is no money or no safe place to raise the child. Nobody is happy about undergoing one, but sometimes it is the best option for a woman. That decision, like a woman's body, is hers alone, and ought not be open to public debate.

Suddenly the pain became virtually unbearable, which again made me want to vomit. My pyjamas were stained bright and dark red around my crotch, bleeding through the sanitary towel, and I could feel small amounts of blood drip down the inside of my leg. I sat on the toilet, the cat screaming at me again and circling my legs, and I stripped my bottoms off which were wet, and heavy with blood. Then the diarrhoea started and I coughed and spluttered as I felt intense amounts of liquid and wet matter spill out of me. The urge to vomit suddenly returned and I thought back to the medicine's directions—is this too much pain—and I jumped up from the toilet seat to lean over the sink.

I sobbed loudly as I wretched and the cat's meows became even more intense, and as I leaned back to wipe my face I saw it on the rug beneath my feet. A bundle of what looked like liver, dark red, streaked with tiny bits of white and grey, a neat pile of matter in a small pool of dark blood. There it was on the mat, slowly the stain around it grew as I stared at this grape- sized organism, the source of all this pain, finally expelled from my body. I stared in awe and disgust at it, saddened and worn and elated that it was over, all at the same time. My legs were now covered in huge streaks of browning blood and I rubbed the cat to settle her down before walking off to find new bottoms.

My boyfriend came in drunk to the bathroom and shouted disgustedly at me for staining the mat and then abruptly left again. I returned to the sitting room, a bit tear streaked and put the mat and ruined things into the bin. As I sat gently down on the sofa he jumped up and in the tone of a moody teenager went on an angry diatribe of how 'nobody thought about how this effected him' before retiring to bed in a strop. I lay on the sofa shivering, unsure of whether to take the next dose or not, staring into space with the cat nuzzled up and purring at my belly. One thing for sure, however, was that not having a child with a massively selfish man baby was the only option for me.

Three days later, still in a severe amount of pain, but needing the money, I returned to work with a severely nerve in my back. Once again, I didn't have another option.

[tHe DaY tHe FiFtY eUrO wEnT oN fIrE oN a CaNdLe HaIkU]

fuck fuck fuck fuck fuck,

fuck fuck fuck fuck fuck fuck fuck,

fuck fuck fuck fuck fuck.

ThE dEvll'S dOoRbEll

Recent studies have shown that women in heterosexual couples orgasm way less than the guys – as few as one for every three that their male partners have in fact. This is complicated further by the fact that 86% of women in lesbian couples have orgasms most or all of the time (all sourced down the end of this article anyway). I don't know if that is surprising to anyone, particularly people with vaginas, but if it is, maybe we need to have a look at some of the sexual constructs that uphold this crap – because we all deserve orgasms, don't we?

For the life of me I cannot work out if the phrase the 'devil's doorbell' is actually real, or not. Just in case you weren't aware of it- it's the clitoris – and in the context of extreme Christian religion seems believable. So is that why it seems that women are having sex but not getting their doorbells rang? Because their enjoyment is seen as shameful, or at least secondary? Sure, let's have a look, wha?

Don't get me wrong – this isn't a big bash on men here – we know that women get stuff wrong too – but if porn has taught me anything – and well, real life too, women have been conditioned to be givers and our orgasm is secondary to that of the man's pleasure. It's totally true. I've had so many experiences over the course of my life that once the dude is done the sex ends there without even a question of how that worked out for ya. I also recently watched a video where men were asked a lot about their last sexual experience. They were asked if they came to which they answered 'yes', but when asked about the woman they banged they either said 'I think so' or 'I don't know'. Seriously?!

I think women have been conditioned to just be passive about the whole thing and not ask for what they want. I remember a guy saying to me 'sure it's normal women don't cum every time, yeah?' when I pointed out that I wanted more than one substandard ride a week that never worked out for me. That didn't last very long – I'll tell you that – especially when the softest direction on how to improve my 'time' was met with hostility because of their fragile fucking ego.

Look, I get it – sex education is a load of arse – and focuses on the rudimentary functions – penis gets hard, goes in, cums, goes out. So the emphasis is on the penis and the penis having a good time so it can yack in the lady parts to make a baby. But what about the lady having fun? Surely, it's important for everyone to have fun or do people just want women to pretend they're having fun (and believe me lots of women do this just to get it over with)? Please don't say 'I've never had any complaints' either because we (well not me) are as polite as fuck and know it's a sensitive issue.

I will concede here that not all women can cum, but you can't assume we won't. You know maybe ask us what you could do to help us along maybe. It seems like communication about sex is just based on a lot of assumptions that no news is good news. So guys keep thinking the riding is adequate, our enthusiasm wanes and nothing gets said. There's two peeps in it but you don't want to make people feel shit and ruin any potential future boners either. Seriously, I know this is terrible to say but there have been several things that I kept going with dudes that I actually didn't like and had nothing else going for them particularly just because they were so good at riding – so you know upping your game improves your situation vastly – although I'm a bit of a messed up person so that mightn't be a great example.

OK so what I've done here is start a group chat where 8 of us tried to come up with a list of things that universally appealed to us and advice that we would give men. You'd think some of these were obvious but apparently they're not. I shall also include anonymous quotes because I was in bits laughing.

1: Be careful sucking that clit – it ain't a straw – it's a tiny bundle of nerve endings – and that can hurt.

2: Please avoid mashing your nose into the pubic bone or that general area for the love of God.

3: Do not expect loads of blowies if you're not reciprocating.

'Some are better with their mouth than their fingers and vice versa. But no way in well would I go down on a guy if he refused to go down on me. Tit for tat baby.'

and

'I think loads of men are actually kind of crap at going down – well actually, no I don't – I think they are deliberately crap at it so they don't get asked to do it again.'

4: Do not attempt entry if there is no wetness. Sometimes that hurts, and can even rip things. Foreplay is very important and should not be stopped after you've banged a few times:

'Like, some guys seem to think that when they get you off a few times they've got the cheat code, and will try to run through the same routine as quickly as possible until they can get their dick wet. Keep exploring, having playful fun, It's not

*"kiss the neck, honk the boobs twice, slurp on the clit and
horse it in."'*

5: Do not assume because you're done that this is done. You have a
face and hands yeah?

*Also- if I don't get off, I very much consider him to still be on
the clock. We aren't done until we're both done so if he comes
and I'm still working on it, I expect assistance.*

6: Do check and see if stuff is working out for us. I know this sounds
obvious but sometimes we're being super polite. I'm sure you'll
know if it's working to an extent but at least saying something can
open it up to us saying 'actually left a bit' or 'down' or 'harder'.

7: There is a fine line with sexy talk. It can be great or cheese or too
much depending on what you're into. We seemed to overall find that
it didn't work as well with one night stands. Also, putting people on
the spot with it is super off putting.

*'Sexy talk isn't efficient for a one night thing, in my experience.
It's cool when you know someone and know what they're into
and vice versa but it's too risky with a stranger. What if I say
"talk to me" And then he calls me ma or something? Nope.'*

and

*'I like Sexy talk done well. I love hearing a guy tell me how
hard I make him and how he loves my pussy. I like him to tell
me what feels good and I'll do the same for him - it's the only
way to build up to amazing sex.'*

and

'Once when I ended up trying it I'd over thought it waaaaay too much and I just ended up saying 'OH YOU'RE A STAR', which made me laugh so much my horn went away.'

8: Open up for communication a bit better and actually listen to us. If we give you advice listen to it and take it on board because if we're actually telling you to do something we mean it a lot stronger than it is coming across. Don't fucking freak out when we tell you what you're doing isn't working.

'I told a dude that was fingering me that it was hurting me and tried to guide his hand to do things in a way I would actually enjoy. He grabbed his hand back off me and shouted I KNOW WHAT IM DOING! and proceeded to tear the box off me and gave me a UTI.'

and

'Oh yeah, there was another dude who used to do this twisty thing when fingering and rub his knuckles really hard over sensitive bits. And he would get really sulky and moody if I told him to stop mangling my vag'.

9: If something isn't working for the love of Jesus tell us.

'I spent 45 minutes sucking a guy off before and it wasn't going anywhere. My jaw was fucking killing me but he didn't lose his boner so I was confused. I would've appreciated it if he actually had tried to stay in the moment as well as he was watching Countdown the entire time.'

10: Consistency is super important. There is nothing worse than a constant change of rhythm (I'm sure it's the same for guys) and that can literally ruin orgasms. I suggested the following technique (for anything involving rhythm – be it oral, penetrative, or hand stuff) to my buddies which was met with approval across the board: find a thing she's reacting to well, keep doing that exactly – do not change it at all, increase pressure and speed slightly until HEY PRESTO (orgasm!)

11: Do not ask her to act like she's enjoying herself. If she isn't ask why not? Unless you're paying her, in which case, I guess it doesn't really matter.

12: Stay in the moment. It's off putting getting a hand job from someone looking off into the distance.

13: If you want anal only lube will do and don't expect anything without it.

'And a curse forever on the creeper who once poured hair conditioner onto my dry asshole with no kind of consultation.'

14: Please only slobber on our gees. Nowhere else.

15: Just because you've a big dick it doesn't mean you've an excuse to be lazy or that you are automatically a good ride.

16: Don't assume you can just do what you want and we'll be OK with it:

'I had a dude slap me across the face when he came. It was weird. That was a one night thing.'

and

'I had one guy randomly grab my hair and yank it hard with no warning. .. that was painful and took me right out of it. I know some women like it.. but I feel that's something that needs to be discussed. I'm no prude… I totally get the pain pleasure thing… but boundaries need to be be discussed first

and

'The guy who- when I moved, intending to switch positions (I said something like "wait let me just move over"), so I slid myself up the bed and he just pulled me back down to where I'd been before, by my hips. I had to proper yell at him before he'd listen.'

17: Don't openly compare us or even imply that you are to other people you've rode. Especially when you don't put in any effort.

'There was this guy I used to ride and he'd talk about how all his exes were boring in bed. I used to ride him. The common denominator was him. I mean he was literally one out of like three people in my life that I had fuck all chemistry with in bed, yet I still felt like I was being compared to the weird expectations of a super lazy dude and that in turn put me under pressure to try and compare and completely ruined any chance I had of an orgasm.'

18: Don't assume you can just fuck someone's face from the offset:

'Yeah calm your tits there Mick, I need my oesophagus.'

19: Vibrating cock rings are awesome and mean that you don't have to use your hands on the lady parts during riding. Although we found that we're all super different as regards where we orgasm from – be it clitoral, g-spot or cervix.

20: There seemed to be a bit shame from a few of us about our interests – which welcomely came up – and were extremely diverse – almost like we were real people or something, with different needs. Who would've thought it eh? One person admitted to trying things they were ashamed of to which was met by:

'Don't be ashamed ever! Sure there's some people that wanna get into nappies like.'

A massive factor that also contributed to our enjoyment of sex was also tied in with how we felt about ourselves and our bodies. We can be sensitive little creatures about these matters so we can – even if we like getting choked, pegging or squirt all over the place. Although there is undeniably pressure on men and women about their physical appearance, there is considerably more on women, and as a result, we can feel the impact of what is expected on a societal level on us. Not only are men allowed to under-preform in the bedroom, but we are also expected to look better than they do and be happy about getting the chance to fuck some mediocre dick.

So the 'devil's doorbell' seems like quite a paradox in that it involves shaming women for tempting men and themselves but when we get down to the actual facts, the statistics show that women in straight relationships aren't having as many orgasms. So that seems to indicate to me that we're just as horny but that our pleasure isn't as recognised. Decent fulfilling relationships, particularly on the physical side, certainly involve partnership, communication and awareness and these figures definitely indicate otherwise. Women's pleasure has always appeared second to that of men's (if at all), and whilst that is nobody's direct fault, it needs to be addressed instead of perpetuated. Women need to voice their needs, and men need to actively participate.

So can we all be humans about this? I don't think it's difficult to give someone else an orgasm is it? Do you not want to give other people pleasure and get repeat rides like? We're all self conscious. We're all assholes. We should demand equality in all things. Including orgasms. Because although they're not the be-all-and-end-all of sexy times they should be a prerequisite for everyone. The more effort you put in the more we probably will.[1]

And c'mon, that doorbell isn't gonna press itself like...

---

[1] https://www.cbsnews.com/news/orgasm-gap-sex-study- straight-women-have-fewer-orgasms-than-men/

ArE yOu a MeNz QuIz?

So are you a 'menz'? It's different than a man – which on its own I have no issue with. 'Menz', however, are different and live in their own little world of toxic masculinity which perpetuates their own misery and this misery leads to sadz… which leads to menz tears… which is the main source of my feminist power.

Here's a quiz to see how menzy you are. On their own loads of these aren't that bad but when cumulatively applied and a high score is reached you're probably not my kind of person.

They're simple yes or no, with one point awarded for each yes. If you score over 35 let me know because your tears will taste exquisite.

1: Do you like to be controversial for the sake of it?

2: Do you make shit jokes about vegetarians that weren't even funny 10 years ago?

3: Do you rely on the women in your life for emotional support that you wouldn't with the male counterparts you know?

4: Do you start sentences regularly with 'women are'?

5: Do you often start explaining things to women without gauging their level of expertise first (or even despite knowing that this IS their area of expertise or job)?

6: Do you make a point of talking to women about their pleasure being important to you like it's exceptional?

7: Do you go asleep without checking if your partner has also orgasmed?

8: The female body is a mystery yeah?

9: Do you believe it's weak for men to cry?

10: Have you ever referred to yourself as 'woke'?

11: Do you belittle, even subtly, women's looks, personality or intellect when chatting them up?

12: Do you think women talk too much?

13: Do you think women talk more than men?

14: Do you think 'rape culture' is a myth?

15: Do you think Jordan Peterson is cool?

16: In a public setting do you feel the need to talk loudly and over everybody?

17: Do public displays of affection bother you?

18: Do public displays or affection bother you when it's not a heterosexual couple?

19: Are gay men gross but lesbians hot?

20: Do you treat your mother like shit?

21: Have you ever referred to your partner as 'a ball and chain', or something to that effect?

22: Do you feel the need to tell women your opinion on their physical appearance without prompting?

23: It is often negative?

24: Have you ever lied to get sex?

25: Have you ever 'accidentally' put your dick in the wrong hole?

26: Would you be pissed off if you only had daughters?

27: If you had a son (or have one) would you speak to him about consent?

28: Do you think women are worse to each other than men are to women?

29: All women are after the same thing?

30: Are you scared of men seeing your dick?

31: Are you afraid to hug other men?

32: Have you ever said 'where are all the female {insert career dominated by men here}?'

33: Have you ever played devil's advocate about a rape case?

34: Is a woman farting gross but a man farting OK?

35: After you scratch yourself do you smell your hand?

36: Do all women love shoes?

37: There is a fine line between normal and needy, yeah?

38: Have you ever unironically said 'not all men'?

39: When a woman or women have been discussing something relevant to them through statistics and/or experience have you said 'what about the men' or 'that happens to men too', or 'I don't do that.'

40: Would you laugh at a friend that was being physically abused by a female partner?

41: Do you have difficulty expressing emotion with words?

42: Do you have a hard time listening to women?

43: Have you ever had sex with someone who was waayyy drunker than you?

44: Do you think the amount of sexual partners a woman has had can have an impact on her vag?

45: If someone laughed during sex would you freak out?

46: Have you ever explained men to women by saying 'this is what men do?'

47: Do men have higher sex drives than women?

48: Would you refuse to buy tampons for your lady in the supermarket?

49: Do you refuse to go to the doctor until you're super unwell?

50: Do you deserve cookies for basic tasks?

ReSuLtS

0-10:   VErY sLiGhTlY mEnzY

You are probably a nice sensitive dude who writes poetry.
Do you play an instrument by any chance? People would
probably say you're a 'cuck', but you're just sound, and judge
people on an individual basis as opposed to silly gender
stereotypes. You are fully capable of having female friends
that you don't want to ride.

11-20: sLiGhTlY mEnzY

I'm going guess that you have at least a passing interest in
sport. You probably think you're 'woke', but you're a bit off
the mark sometimes. You're human though and have done
some questionable things. You have female friends as well,
BUT you rely on them emotionally way more than you would
male friends. If you learned how to play a musical
instrument you did it to get the ride.

21-30: mOdErAtElY mEnzY

You are a bit of an awkward person with women and (even
internally) believe that 'women are…' about a loud of things.
You think it's a compliment to tell women 'they're not like
other girls'. Your primary focus of any friendship with a lady
is to ride them, although you do have female friends, but you
do believe 'the friend zone' is an actual thing. You are a bit

shit at expressing emotions, unless at sport, and probably quite stubborn. You talk over women loads. You make a lot of dick jokes.

31-40: mEnzY mEnz

You have zero female friends and any woman that talks to you is trying it on. You are mostly cranky or angry. You are super obsessed with sport as well and it is the only time that you ever express any real feelings about anything. You do not understand compromise. You are possessive over the poor yoke that you end up with, yet cheat a ridiculous amount on her. You're not 100% sure that you've ever made someone cum now that you think about it. Lesbians are cool but gay men are gross. You're kinda scared of gay men to be honest, but probably only because you're frightened that they'll treat you the way you treat women.

41-50: uBeR mEnz

Your tears will taste delicious and fuel me for days on end. The world literally revolves around you. You are unable to give a compliment or show support. Despite your cranky outward nature you are actually a glorified man child. Perhaps you disappear for days on benders and lie about where you've been whilst your partner minds your kid, perhaps you feel the need to tell women that they're fat, perhaps you've even hit a woman, but you definitely don't have the emotional awareness to actually be in a proper relationship with other humans. You probably love the film 'Scar Face' and make jokes about vegetarianism that weren't even funny ten years ago.

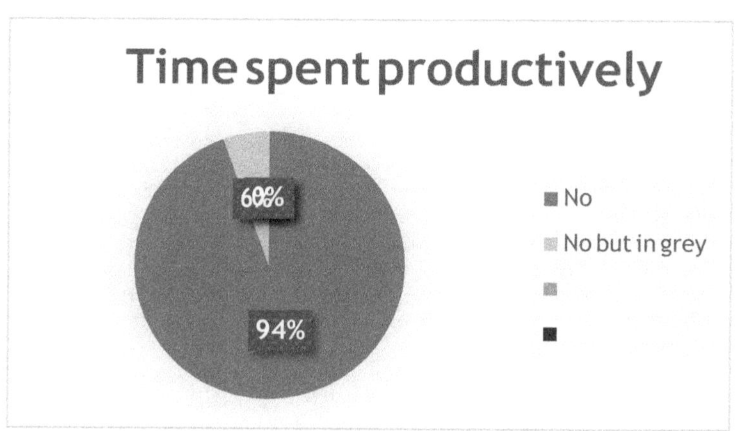
Time spent productively
No
No but in grey
60%
94%

Even more hair everywhere
How I know I'm getting old
Loud places make me afraid
Midnight seems late
People in their 20's confuse me

ThE sHuT tHe FuCk Up ChArT

Worried about whether you should talk? This handy chart will help you figure out how to not be a complete dope.

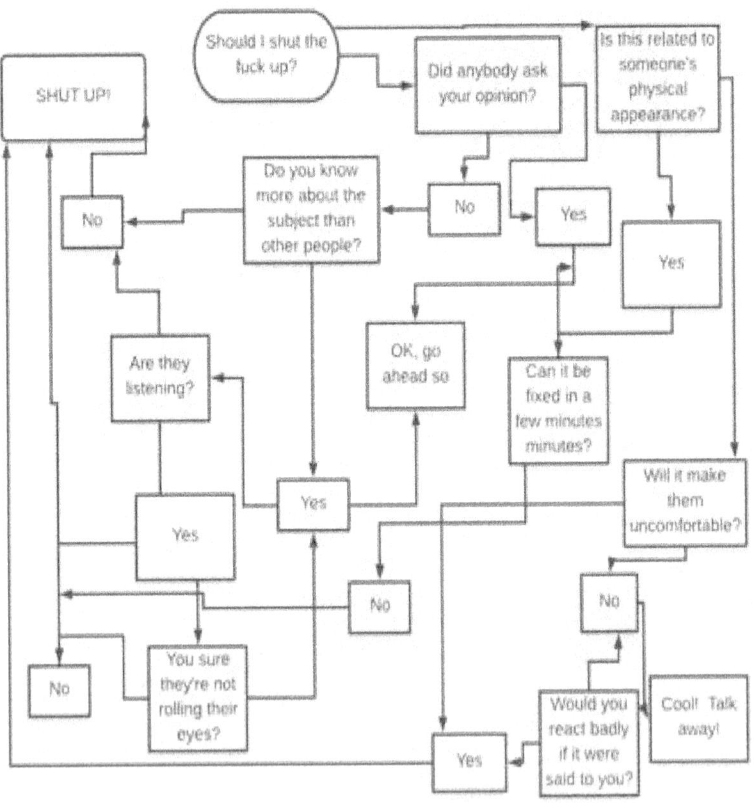

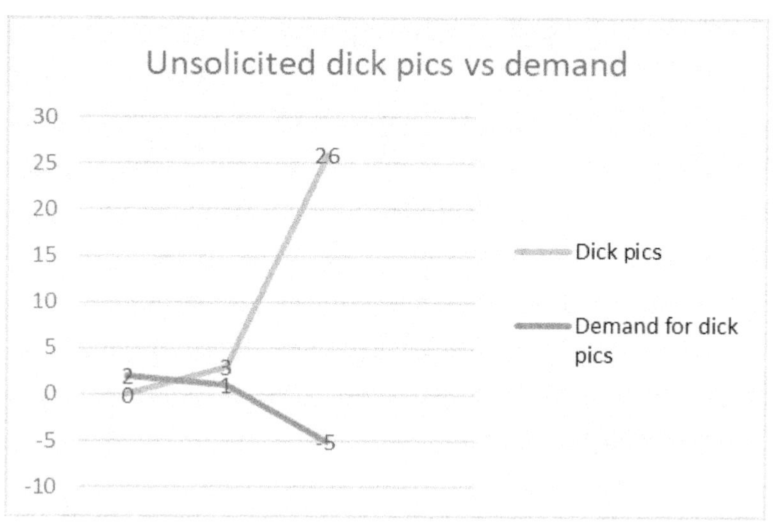

Unsolicited dick pics vs demand
30
25
20
15
10
5
0
-5
-10
26
2
0
3
1
-5
Dick pics
Demand for dick pics

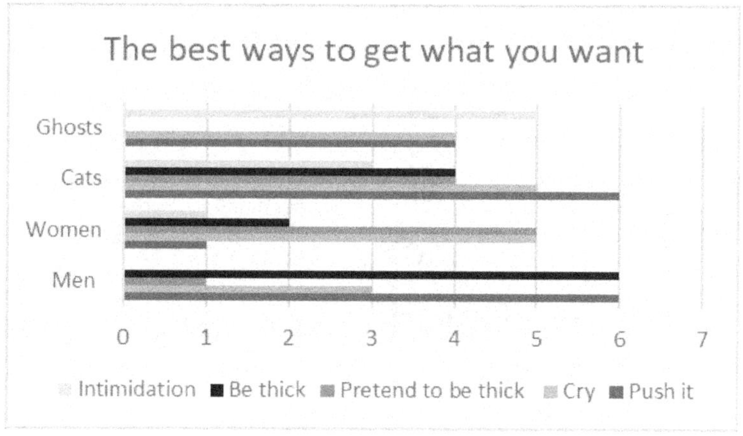

The best ways to get what you want
Ghosts
Cats
Women
Men
0
1
2
3
4
5
6
7
Intimidation
Be thick
Pretend to be thick
Cry
Push it

ReAl LiFe PrIoRiTs

Teens

Sex

Fun

Sleep

20s

Sex

Fun

Sleep

30's

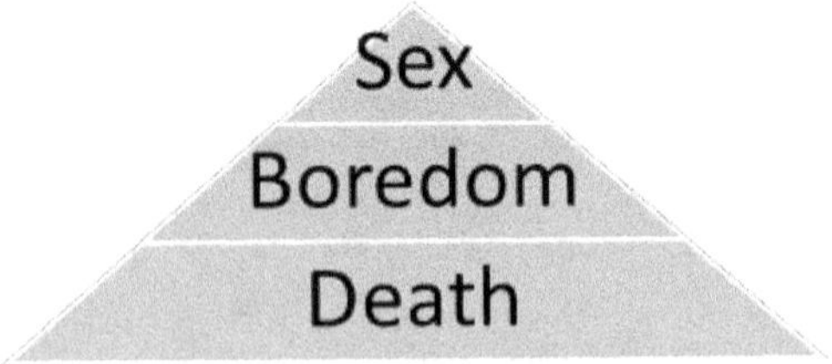

Sex

Boredom

Death

I dOn'T kNoW tHeY jUsT lOoK cOoL

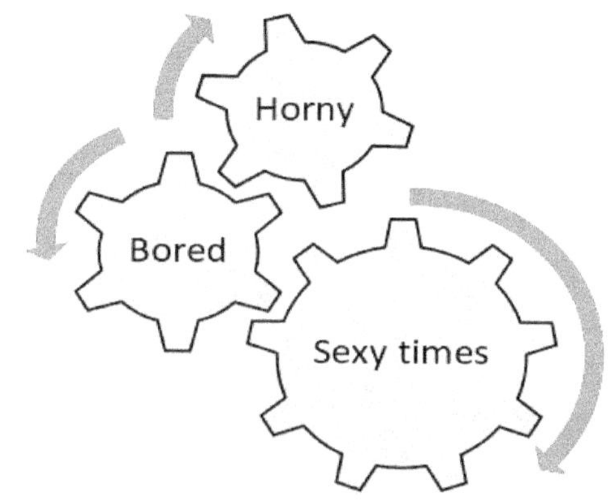

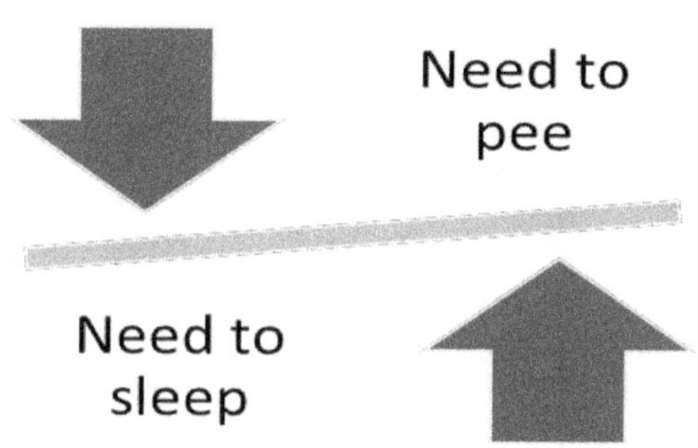

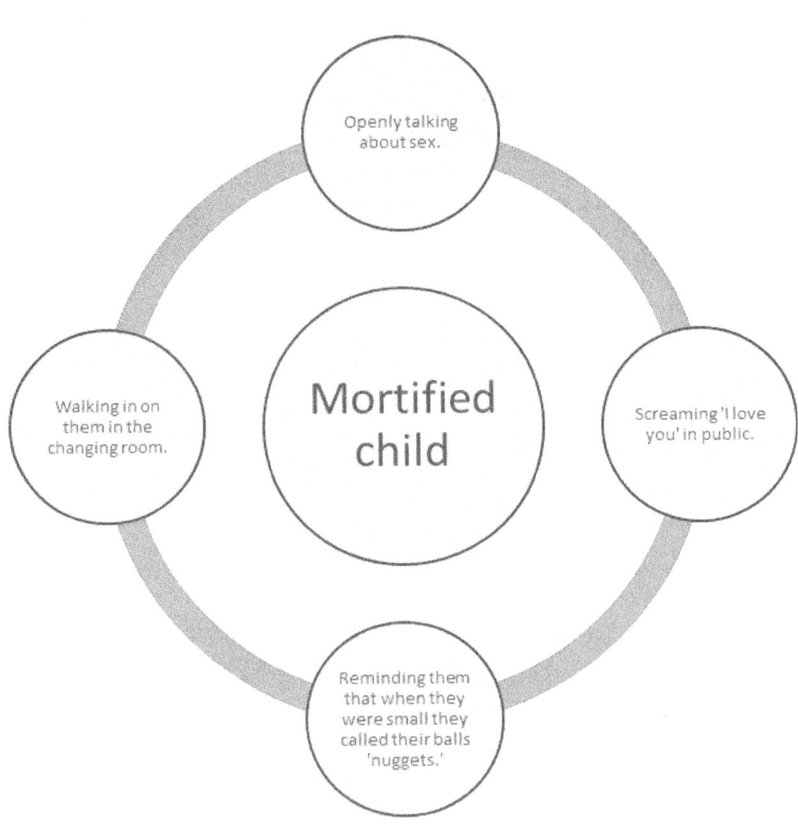
Openly talking about sex.
Mortified child
Walking in on them in the changing room.
Screaming 'I love you' in public.
Reminding them that when they were small they called their balls 'nuggets.'

aBoUt ThE aUtHoR

Theorizing that one could time travel within her own lifetime, Dr. Caroline Egan led an elite group of scientists into the desert to develop a top-secret project, known as "Fahckmylife." Pressured to prove her theories or lose funding, Dr. Egan prematurely stepped into the Project Accelerator--and vanished.

She awoke to find herself in the past, suffering from partial amnesia and facing a mirror image that was not her own. Fortunately, contact with her own time was maintained through brainwave transmissions with AI, the Project Observer, who appeared in the form of a hologram that only Dr. Egan could see and hear. Trapped in the past, Dr. Egan finds herself leaping from life to life, putting things right that once went wrong and hoping each time that her next leap will be the leap home.

You can find more of my stuff here:

www.fahckmylife.com

Facebook: Caroline Egan Writer

Instagram: cacababy13

YouTube: Fahckmylife podcast

Previous book Fahckmylife: The Little Book of Fahck is available on Amazon and Createspace

Notes: